easy going
locker zu super Noten

Schulaufgaben

von bayerischen Gymnasien

Englisch 9

mit Lösungen

DURCHBLICKER
Lernstudio Arndt

Schulaufgaben von bayerischen Gymnasien

Verfügbare Titel

☺ **Mathematik** für Klasse **5, 6, 7, 8, 9, 10, 11** und **12**

☺ **Physik** für Klasse **8, 9** und **10**

☺ **Chemie** für Klasse **8, 9** und **10**

☺ **Englisch** für Klasse **5, 6, 7, 8, 9, 10** und **11/12**

☺ **Französisch** für Klasse **6, 7, 8** und **9**

☺ **Deutsch** für Klasse **5, 6, 7** und **8**

☺ **Latein** für Lernjahr **1, 2** und **3**

Schulaufgaben bayerischer Realschulen

Verfügbare Titel

☺ **Mathematik** für Klasse **5, 6, 7II / III, 8II / III, 9II / III** und **10II / III**

☺ **Englisch** für Klasse **5, 6, 7, 8, 9** und **10**

☺ **Deutsch** für Klasse **5, 6, 7** und **8**

Schulproben von bayerischen Mittelschulen

Verfügbare Titel

☺ **Mathematik** für Klasse **5** und **6**

☺ **Englisch** für Klasse **5** und **6**

☺ **Deutsch** für Klasse **5** und **6**

Schulproben von bayerischen Grundschulen

Verfügbare Titel

☺ **Mathematik** für Klasse **3** und **4**

☺ **Deutsch** für Klasse **3** und **4**

☺ **Heimat- und Sachunterricht (HSU)** für Klasse **3** und **4**

Vorwort

Liebe Schüler, liebe Eltern,

seit der G8-Reform zur Verkürzung der Schulzeit ist Englisch praxisnäher und lebendiger geworden. Diese

Schulaufgaben von bayerischen Gymnasien

Englisch 9

zeigen, welche Aufgabentypen und welcher Schwierigkeitsgrad im G8-Gymnasium in Bayern verlangt werden. Ein großer Teil der Aufgaben habe ich als Englischlehrerin selber entworfen. Original-Schulaufgaben von Nachhilfeschülern unseres ***Durchblicker Lernstudio Arndt*** bilden die Grundlage der Aufgaben in diesem Buch. Wer diese Schulaufgaben konsequent durcharbeitet, dem sind bessere Noten sicher. Durch Übung kommt jeder Schüler zum Erfolg.

In der 9. Klasse werden drei Schulaufgaben geschrieben. Oft heißen diese dann „Großer Leistungstest". Im vorliegenden Band finden sich pro Schulaufgabe jeweils zwei Prüfungen. Die sechs hier gestellten Schulaufgaben mit Lösungen entsprechen dem hohen Niveau aus Gymnasien in Bayern, die das

Schülerbuch Green Line New 5

im Unterricht verwenden und auf tatsächlich gestellten Aufgaben basieren. Als Schüler kennst du ***Vocabulary*** mit Übungen zu Vokabeln und ***Grammar*** mit Übungen zur Grammatik. ***Speaking*** lernst du zum Training der Sprachfertigkeit. ***Writing*** übst du durch ***Dictation*** und schulst das Schreiben mit Diktatübungen. ***Dialogue*** und ***Mediation*** dient zur Übersetzung ins Englische. ***Reading Comprehension*** fördert das Textverständnis. ***Listening Comprehension*** verbessert das Hörverstehen.

Mit diesem Band kannst du Schritt für Schritt alle Schulaufgaben durcharbeiten, bis du fit bist für die nächste Schulaufgabe. Wenn der Lehrer eine Schulaufgabe ankündigt, sagt er z.B. von Unit 1 bis einschließlich Unit 2, dann solltest du die entsprechenden Schulaufgaben üben. Versuche die Aufgaben selbstständig zu lösen wie in einer richtigen Schulaufgabe. Gibt es einen Hörtext im Lösungsteil, lass dir den Text zweimal vorlesen. Vergleiche deine Lösungen mit den Lösungen der Schulaufgaben und korrigiere dich selbst. Wenn sich die Fehler häufen, dann musst du verstärkt Vokabeln lernen oder in der Grammatik oder im Schülerbuch noch einmal die Kapitel, um die es geht, wiederholen.

Mein Ziel ist es, die Motivation und Kreativität aller Schüler beim Lösen von Schulaufgaben in Englisch zu fördern. Dazu biete ich die **ausführliche Lösung** der Aufgabenstellung an.

Viel Spaß beim Lösen der Schulaufgaben

Deine und Ihre Englischtrainerin Monika Arndt

Monika Arndt (Dipl.-Übersetzerin), veröffentlichte als Buchautorin Ernährungsbücher für Kinder in den Verlagen dtv und Ravensburger. **Das Baby-Kochbuch**, **Wie Kinder fit und gesund bleiben** und **Das Ravensburger Kochbuch für Kinder** mit Bildern von Ali Mitgutsch.
Zuvor hat Monika Arndt in verschiedenen Redaktionen gearbeitet, z.B. über zehn Jahre in der Redaktion des Schulfernsehheftes beim Bayerischen Schulfernsehen. Beim Stark-Verlag hat sie über Produktion und Inhalt von Lernhilfen Erfahrungen gesammelt, geeignete Lehrer gesucht und die Bücher als Lektorin redigiert.
Sie unterrichtet Englisch und Französisch im ***Durchblicker Lernstudio Arndt***.

Wir danken Mike Cross, der diesen Band kritisch durchgesehen hat.
Titelbild: Heinrich Schmid, Überlingen am Ried / Singen am Hohentwiel
www.durchblicker.org

ISBN **978-3-943703-09-2**

ISBN 978-3-943703-09-2
9 783943 703092 >

1. Schulaufgabe aus dem Englischen

Name: ___________________________

Stoff: Unit 1–2

I. Listening Comprehension *(Text aus Lösung 2x vorlesen lassen)*

Listen to the following text twice. Afterwards answer the questions

1. Answer these questions by ticking off the correct answer

	true	false	not in text
Laura wants to study law.			
Mr Milton is her boss.			
Mr Miller is a close family friend.			
Mr Furton likes Laura.			
Her boss is very nice.			
He offers her coffee from the cafeteria.			
Laura has to collect copies and letters at the front desk.			
Laura is going to study law after school.			
Laura's mum thinks it would be great if she studied law.			

2. Tick off the correct answer

a) Laura doesn't have any ○ computer skills ○ friends ○ work to do.

b) Laura's boss ○ thinks she's interesting ○ wants her to work for the firm ○ loses interest in her.

c) Laura's father ○ wants her to study law ○ doesn't want her to study law ○ doesn't care if she studies law or not.

d) Mr Miller ○ thinks studying law is great ○ thinks studying law isn't great.

e) At the law firm Laura ○ has fun ○ is bored ○ enjoys her time ○ can't do much.

II. Grammar

1. An interview with Geoff Rowley
Put the correct verb forms
o Mixed tenses (simple and progressive) forms: present, present perfect, past, past perfect
o Gerund and Infinitives (add to where necessary and find the correct preposition for *prep*)

Interviewer: High Geoff. We ________________ (see) you a lot on TV over the last few years.

Geoff: That's right. I ________________ (work) a lot at the moment. But I also enjoy ______________________ (meet) my fans.

Interviewer: When ______________________ (you o start) your career?

Geoff: I ______________________ (begin o skate) at the age of four.

Interviewer: Is it true that you like the idea ___________________ (*prep* o push) your limits?

Geoff: Yes, of course. And I ______________________________ (not o mind o do) the same tricks again and again until I'm perfect. Yesterday I _________________ (stay) at the skate park until 10 p.m. All my friends ________________________ (go) to the pub by then. They ______________________ (play) pool while I ____________________ (still o skate).

Interviewer: I see. ___________________ (be) successful _______________________ (mean o work) hard. Everybody can do it!

Geoff: Well, I guess it's not possible for everyone ___________________________ (be good o *prep* o skate) – just as I'm a useless musician. I remember _________________ (tell) a friend of mine: "You ___________________________ (play) the piano for only one year now and you could already apply to the National Orchestra. I could never do that. Don't forget ____________________ (invite) me to your first concert!"

2. Choose the correct verb form! Sometimes you must tick two underlined sentences because both forms are correct. Tick the correct circles (○ like this: ⊗)

Interviewer: Let's turn to your plans for the future. When ○ <u>are we able</u> / ○ <u>will we be able</u> / ○ <u>are we be going to be able</u> to see your next show?

Geoff: Well, tonight – if you want. The show ○ starts / ○ is starting / ○ is going to start at 8:30.

Thousands of fans, good tricks, good music – it ○ 's /○'s going to be / ○ 'll be a lot of fun for all of us.

Interviewer: Great! And after the show? ○ Are you having / ○ Are you going to have / ○ Do you have any plans?

Geoff: ○ I'm having / ○ I have / ○ I'm going to have a big party: I've invited lots of fans and friends.

3. Gerund or infinitive? Translate these sentences into English. Use either the gerund or the infinitive form

a) Möchtest du einen Film mit mir anschauen?

____

____

b) Ich bin mir nicht sicher. Ich glaube, ich würde lieber ein Buch lesen.

____

____

c) Ich habe aufgehört Kekse zu machen.

____

____

d) Ich habe aufgehört, um Kekse zu machen.

____

____

e) Vergiss nicht deine Mutter anzurufen!

____

____

f) Ich werde nie vergessen, wie ich mit Oma skifahren war.

____

____

III. Vocabulary

1. Say in other words
Explain these vocabulary words in complete sentences

a) content: 1. (singular): ____

____

2. (plural): ____

____

b) to mean to do sth: ____

____

____

c) craftsman: ____

____

2. Opposites: Give the opposite of the given word and translation of both words

a) to reduce sth ⇔ ____

Translation: ______________________________ ⇔ ____________________

c) to attack ⇔ ____

Translation: ______________________________ ⇔ ____________________

d) to pick sb. up ⇔ ____

Translation: ______________________________ ⇔ ____________________

3. Working in a globalised world
Complete the text with the missing (new) words. The first letters are given

It is true to say that working co_____________ have changed dramatically over the past few years. On the one hand, technological de____________________ have made work more comfortable and more e________________. Computers give us ac___________ to huge databases. Mo____________________ has increased thanks to faster means of tr_________________ like high speed trains and airplanes.
On the other hand, it has become easy for big co________________ to produce their goods in de_________________ countries where w________________ are low. Charity organisations have been complaining for a long time about the way workers are ex________________.
Even children have to work long sh_________.

What is more, the job market has become highly com_______________. Only the best can succeed. You have to choose your ca___________ very carefully. Make sure that you are su_____________ to the job you want to work in, but be also ready to meet the ch__________________ of today's globalised world.

IV. Opinion

What about a gap year?

Gap years have been popular in Britain and the USA for a long time and not only because of Prince Harry who went to Africa in 2004
Would you like to do a gap Year? Say why / why not!
In your answer mention two advantages and two disadvantages of doing a gap year
Give one good example of a gap year programme
Write a coherent (zusammenhängend) well-structured text
Write about 120 words. Use an extra sheet of paper

Good luck !

Lösung: 1. Schulaufgabe aus dem Englischen

I. Listening Comprehension *(Text 2x vorlesen lassen)*

Listen to the following text. Afterwards answer the questions

Laura wanted to do an internship at a local law firm. She was thinking about studying law at university yet wasn't completely sure if that was what she wanted. Her mother encouraged her to do so. Her father wasn't sure if it was the right choice for Laura because she had never liked learning things by heart. His friend Mr Miller was a lawyer and had told him that the studies were really rough. Milton, a close family friend encouraged Laura to do the internship. He was working at a law firm in town and helped her get the internship.

When Laura started on the first day she met with her boss Mr Furton. He was the one she was going to follow around to see how things were done. Laura was very enthusiastic about helping but had to learn that there wasn't much she could do. She was sent to the front desk sometimes to collect letters or important copies or to the cafeteria to buy coffee for Mr Furton. He had asked her if she had any computer skills and when Laura said no he had lost interest in her. Working for him was a nightmare and Laura complained to her parents every night. Her father liked that Laura didn't have fun while her mother petted Laura's head every night telling her it was still good to get the insight into the workspace.

After two weeks Laura was happy when her internship was over. She promised herself that she would still think about studying law in college. Being a lawyer is a great opportunity to help people, she thought.

1. Answer these questions by ticking off the correct answer

	true	**false**	**not in text**
Laura wants to study law.	*x*		
Mr Milton is her boss.		*x*	
Mr Miller is a close family friend.		*x*	
Mr Furton likes Laura.			*x*
Her boss is very nice.		*x*	
He offers her coffee from the cafeteria.		*x*	
Laura has to collect copies and letters at the front desk.	*x*		
Laura is going to study law after school.			*x*
Laura's mum thinks it would be great if she studied law.	*x*		

____/9

2. Tick off the correct answer

a) Laura doesn't have any ⊗ computer skills O friends O work to do.

b) Laura's boss O thinks she's interesting O wants her to work for the firm ⊗ loses interest in her.

c) Laura's father O wants her to study law ⊗ doesn't want her to study law O doesn't care if she studies law or not.

d) Mr Miller O thinks studying law is great ⊗ thinks studying law isn't great.

e) At the law firm Laura O has fun O is bored O enjoys her time ⊗ can't do much.

____/5

II. Grammar

1. An interview with Geoff Rowley
Put the correct verb forms
o Mixed tenses (simple and progressive) forms: present, present perfect, past, past perfect
o Gerund and Infinitives (add to where necessary and find the correct preposition for *prep*)

Interviewer: High Geoff. We*'ve seen* (see) you a lot on TV over the last few years.

Geoff: That's right. I*'m working* (work) a lot at the moment. But I also enjoy *meeting* (meet) my fans.

Interviewer: When *did you start* (you o start) your career?

Geoff: I *began skating* (begin o skate) at the age of four.

Interviewer: Is it true that you like the idea *of pushing* (***prep*** o push) your limits?

Geoff: Yes, of course. And I *don't mind doing* (not o mind o do) the same tricks again and again until I'm perfect. Yesterday I *stayed* (stay) at the skate park until 10 p.m. All my friends *had gone* (go) to the pub by then. They *were playing* (play) pool while I *was still skating* (still o skate).

Interviewer: I see. *Being* (be) successful *means working* (mean o work) hard. Everybody can do it!

Geoff: Well, I guess it's not possible for everyone *to be good at skating* (be good o ***prep*** o skate) – just as I'm a useless musician. I remember *having told* (tell) a friend of mine: "You*'ve been playing* (play) the piano for only one year now and you could already apply to the National Orchestra. I could never do that. Don't forget *to invite* (invite) me to your first concert!"

One point for each gap and one point for each correct preposition

____/19

2. Choose the correct verb form! Sometimes you must tick two underlined sentences because both forms are correct. Tick the correct circles (○ like this: ⊗)

Interviewer: Let's turn to your plans for the future. When ○ are we able / ⊗ will we be able / ○ are we be going to be able to see your next show?

Geoff: Well, tonight – if you want. The show ⊗ starts / ○ is starting / ○ is going to start at 8:30. Thousands of fans, good tricks, good music – it ○ 's ⊗ 's going to be ⊗ 'll be a lot of fun for all of us.

Interviewer: Great! And after the show? ○ Are you having / ○ Are you going to have ⊗ Do you have any plans?

Geoff: ⊗ I'm having / ○ I have / ⊗ I'm going to have a big party: I've invited lots of fans and friends.

____/7

3. Gerund or infinitive? Translate these sentences into English. Use either the gerund or the infinitive form

Tipps und Hinweise
– Nach ***would like / love*** wird immer **der Infinitiv** verwendet.
– Nach den **Verben *to begin / to start / to like / to love / to hate / to prefer*** kann sowohl der **Infinitiv** als auch **gerund** verwendet werden. Die Bedeutung bleibt gleich.
– Wird das **gerund** nach *forget* benutzt steht es für eine **Handlung, die schon stattgefunden hat.**
– Wird der **Infinitiv nach** *forget* benutzt steht es für eine **Handlung, die in der Zukunft liegt.**
– Das **gerund nach** ***stop*** bezeichnet die **Handlung, die abgebrochen wird.**
– Der **Infinitiv nach** ***stop*** bezeichnet die **Absicht, etwas Neues zu tun.**

a) Möchtest du einen Film mit mir anschauen?

Would you like to watch a movie / film with me?

b) Ich bin mir nicht sicher. Ich glaube, ich würde lieber ein Buch lesen.

I'm not sure. I think I'd prefer reading / to read a book.

c) Ich habe aufgehört Kekse zu machen.

I stopped making cookies.

d) Ich habe aufgehört, um Kekse zu machen.

I stopped to make cookies.

e) Vergiss nicht deine Mutter anzurufen!

Don't forget to call your mother!

f) Ich werde nie vergessen, wie ich mit Oma skifahren war.

I will never forget skiing with Grandma.

____/6

III. Vocabulary

1. Say in other words
Explain these vocabulary words in complete sentences.

a) content: 1. (singular) *Information or ideas in a book, brochure, film, photo, etc.*

2. (plural) *Everything that is inside something e.g. a box, a bag, a drawer.*

b) to mean to do sth: *If you mean to do something you are planning on doing it.*

c) craftsman: *A person that is using his / her talents and skills to make or create something, usually by hand.*

____/4

2. Opposites: Give the opposite of the given word and translation of both words

a) to reduce sth. ⇔ *to increase sth.*

Translation: *etwas reduzieren* ⇔ *etwas vergrößern*

c) to attack ⇔ *to defend*

Translation: *angreifen* ⇔ *verteidigen*

d) to pick sb. up ⇔ *to drop sb. off*

Translation: *jemanden abholen* ⇔ *jemanden absetzen / aussteigen lassen*

____/9

3. Working in a globalised world
Complete the text with the missing (new) words. The first letters are given

It is true to say that working co*nditions* have changed dramatically over the past few years. On the one hand, technological de*velopments* have made work more comfortable and more e*fficient*. Computers give us ac*cess* to huge databases. Mo*bility* has increased thanks to faster means of tr*ansport* like high speed trains and airplanes.
On the other hand, it has become easy for big co*mpanies* to produce their goods in de*veloping* countries where w*ages* are low. Charity organisations have been complaining for a long time about the way workers are ex*ploited*. Even children have to work long sh*ifts*.

Furthermore, the job market has become highly com*petitive*. Only the best can succeed. You have to choose your ca*reer* very carefully. Make sure that you are su*ited* for the job you want to work in, but be also ready to meet the ch*allenges* of today's globalised world.

____/15

IV. Opinion

What about a gap year?
Gap years have been popular in Britain and the USA for a long time and not only because of Prince Harry who went to Africa in 2004
Would you like to do a gap Year? Say why / why not!
In your answer mention two advantages and two disadvantages of doing a gap year
Give one good example of a gap year programme
Write a coherent (zusammenhängend) well-structured text
Write about 120 words

More and more young adults decide to do a gap year after they finish school. There are various reasons for it and I too would like to do a gap year after I am done with school. Even though gap years are very expensive and you can't go to university right after you graduate high school, gap years are a great opportunity for anyone. During a gap year you can learn a new language or get better at one that you already speak. Furthermore you are able to get to know a different culture and country and you can certainly learn from the people you meet. You could, for example go to Australia and backpack there. It is a wonderful experience and I hope to do it.

Tipps und Hinweise
When listing arguments these linking words can be helpful:
Firstly, Secondly, Lastly, Furthermore, In addition to that, For one thing, Adding to this, Also, On the one hand, On the other hand, However, On the other side, Despite the fact that, Even though, Given the fact that
To conclude or finish your text you might find these helpful:
Summing up, In a nutshell, Concluding, To sum up, Coming to an end, All in all

Read through these introductions / first sentences and say what you like or don't like about them

o Yes, I would do a gap year because I think it is good for my career.
o In my opinion doing a gap year is a great thing.
o I'm not Prince Harry and I will never get as famous as he, but we have one thing in common: doing a gap year. I would like to take part in a gap year programme straight after my A-level exams.
o I myself would really like to do a gap year after having finished school.
o I'm sure you've already heard about the possibility of doing a gap year.

First correct the mistakes then decide which of the following arguments are convincing?

o By travelling around the world you practise speaking English. But doing a gap year is very expensive and I don't want to do volunteer work.

o First of all I want to mention that the idea of taking a gap year is very good.

o Secondly you can make new experiences and develop your personality.

o It's true that a gap year can be expensive but I think that's not a reason not to do it. Young people have enough money to spend it on parties.

What would you say about these conclusions / last sentences?

o To sum up I really like the idea of doing a gap year. Instead of wasting your time after school you can do something good for you and other people.

o All in all I would say that a gap year is really interesting but personally I don't want to do one.

o As you see I'm well prepared for doing my gap year. I can't wait to go!

____/18

Total ____/90

Tipps und Hinweise

Text Production

Before writing

– Brainstorm on the topic. Develop an opinion.
– Write down your opinion of your problem or describe the situation.
– Find facts, examples, etc. to support your opinion (e.g. in form of a mind map).
– Put in a logical order the information which you have found.
– If you are dealing with a controversial subject, think about the opposite position and find arguments to reject it.
– Find a good conclusion.

While writing

– Begin your statement with an introduction to the problem, e.g. in form of a summary of your understanding of the subject.
– Give your opinion.
– Support your opinion with the facts you have found.
– Sum up the problem and your opinion and bring your understatement to a conclusion.

After writing

– Re-read your text. Have you covered the essential points?
– Check if you have observed the rules above.
– Are your arguments convincing to someone who might not agree with you?

1. Schulaufgabe aus dem Englischen

Name: ____________________________

Stoff: Unit 1–2

I. Listening Comprehension *(Text aus Lösung 2x vorlesen lassen)*

Maura Jane is a 19 year old young adult who just came back from her travels. She is on a TV show talking about the past year. Listen yourself and answer the questions asked after

Questions on the text

1. Answer these questions by ticking the right answer. More than one answer can be possible but be careful you only get points if you tick off all the possible answers

Maura Jane is	○ Canadian ○ American ○ German ○ French
Maura travelled to	○ Canada ○ North America ○ South America
Mr Tompson has	○ pigs ○ cows ○ geese ○ hen ○ horses
Maura left in	○ July last year ○June last year ○June two years ago

2. Answer these questions in complete sentences

a) Maura went on a trip to do a gap year. Outline her travel route by writing down the countries / towns / areas / states she went to. Be as specific as possible.
(Example: Eiffel Tower, Paris, France → Berlin, Germany → Hamburg, Germany → Austria)

____

____

____

b) Maura did several jobs while she was travelling the world. Write down the jobs she did. If you have the right order you get an extra point. Write in complete sentences.

____

____

____

____

____

c) Maura met interesting people while travelling around. Write one sentence about each person she met and something you know about them. Write in complete sentences.

II. Vocabulary

1. Give a definition for the following words. Write in complete sentences

a) editorial:

b) couch potato:

c) volunteer:

d) to carry sth. out:

2. Translate these sentences from German to English and from English to German

a) Sie war eine Bewerberin für das Praktikum in der Anwaltskanzlei.

b) She crossed her fingers for him.

c) Sie hat diesen Beruf gewählt, weil sie bedürfigen Menschen helfen will.

d) I took a year off and packed my bags to meet up with my cousin in Delaware.

____

____

III. Grammar

Mary's unusual hobby

In this extract from an article published in the youth magazine "pop up" you will read about Mary's unusual hobby.

1. Fill in the verbs in the correct tense. You will need the progressive form once or twice

"Actually I ________________ (want + always) to play soccer before I ________________ (be) 12", 15-year-old Mary ____________________ (tell) our reporter, Tom, on a sunny day in September. They _______________________ (sit) in a nice café. Tom ________________ (ask) Mary to come and tell him about her unusual hobby. "But as a 12-year-old girl living in a small town I ________________ (have) no chance to find enough girls for our team. My second favourite hobby at that time ____________________ (be) reading books – and it ____________________ (become + now) my number one. I think I _____________________________ (read) about 500 books since I ________________ (start) reading at the age of 5. But back then, I ________________ (do + usually) it in a loud voice. I ________________ (become) pretty good at it later...

2. Gerund or infinitive? Fill in the correct form. Sometimes you need to add a preposition

... I still remember ____________________ (imitate) the voices of the characters in the book. My mother used __________________________ (stop) her housework __________________ (listen) to my words. And she encouraged me __________________ (go on). Another step in my career was my little brother. He never stopped _____________________ (ask) me if I could read something to him. And I gave in, because I enjoyed ____________________ (look at) his big eyes.
One day my neighbour asked me if I was interested ____________________ (read) stories to children at the local hospital. I agreed ________________________ (go) there once a week."

3. Mary is writing in her diary. Fill in the correct verb form. Be careful with the different tenses

"Today _________________ (be) such a wonderful day. I_____________________ (have) so much fun at the interview with Tom. He____________ (be) such a nice man. While I ______ __________________________ (tell) him about my favourite hobby I _________________ (realize) that it really is something good. I ____________________ (be) able to help children and cheer them up and what is there better than _________________ (make) someone smile? I think, in the future I am __________________________ (read) more. I am _____________ __________________ (make) more time for the reading. I think it ______________________ _______________ (be) great.

IV. Text Production

Imagine you are writing for your school's magazine. You are supposed to write about your favourite hobby: making others happy. Write about what you do to make others happy. Write about 120 words
(Use an extra sheet of paper)

Good luck !

Lösung: 1. Schulaufgabe aus dem Englischen

I. Listening Comprehension

Maura Jane is a 19 year old young adult who just came back from her travels. She is on a TV show talking about the past year. Listen yourself and answer the questions asked after ***(2x vorlesen lassen)***

My name is Maura Jane and I am glad to be on the show today. I came back from Canada two weeks ago. I really need to tell you about my wonderful trip there. Well to be correct, it wasn't just a trip – it was a gap year that I did, right after finishing school. I started planning June two years ago and finally started my trip in July last year. I flew into Michigan, USA, and worked as a hostess in this tiny little pub there. After a few weeks of travelling the area I decided I needed to go bigger. I took a bus to New York City and helped at a homeless shelter, there. I was able to stay at Ms Daisy's house. Ms Daisy is a wonderful elderly woman who has a heart as big as the ocean. She recommended the New York Opera to me and so I worked there for three weeks, cleaning up the rooms after the shows.

Once I got tired of all the dirt on the floor I decided to work at a restaurant. Well, let's say a fast-food place. The work there was fun but I knew that I wanted to see more. That's when I took a bus up north all the way to Burlington, New York. I tramped the rest of the way to Niagara Falls and was pleasantly surprised to see their beauty. Once I saw them I knew this was where I wanted to work. I was lucky because they needed some extra hands on "The Maid of Mist", a boat that takes tourists right to the waterfalls and then back to the main land. This job was awesome and I loved it every second long.

After a few months though I knew I had to leave if I wanted to make it a little further north during my travels. I walked across the bridge right there at Niagara Falls and I was in Canada. Here I was able to work on a little farm, helping with the animals about three hours from Niagara Falls. I met the farmer Mr Tompson on my way over the bridge. He was impressed that I was travelling all by myself and offered me the job on his farm. I liked the cows, pigs and hen and working with them yet I wished for horses. After a few weeks with Mr Tompson and his family I decided to go to Toronto. I met another girl from Germany there, Anne, and we stayed together for the rest of the time. We did this and that but mostly went to museums, on trips and enjoyed our time left.

My gap year was amazing and I wouldn't trade it for anything. Every German should do a gap year I recommend you do one, too. At least, think about it.

Questions on the text

1. Answer these questions by ticking the right answer. More than one answer can be possible but be careful you only get points if you tick off all the possible answers

Maura Jane is	○ Canadian ○ American ⊗ German ○ French
Maura travelled to	⊗ Canada ⊗ North America ○ South America
Mr Tompson has	⊗ pigs ⊗ cows ○ geese ⊗ hen ○ horses
Maura left in	⊗ July last year ○June last year ○June two years ago

____/4

2. Answer these questions in complete sentences

a) Maura went on a trip to do a gap year. Outline her travel route by writing down the countries / towns / areas / states she went to. Be as specific as possible.
(Example: Eiffel Tower, Paris, France → Berlin, Germany → Hamburg, Germany → Austria)

Germany → Michigan, USA → New York City, USA → Belmont, New York, USA → Niagara Falls, USA → (three hours away from Niagara Falls) Canada → Toronto, Canada → Germany

____/8

b) Maura did several jobs while she was travelling the world. Write down the jobs she did. If you have the right order you get an extra point. Write in complete sentences.

When Maura came to the USA she worked as a hostess in a tiny pub. Then she helped at a homeless shelter. After that she worked at the New York Opera, cleaning the rooms. Later she worked at a fast-food place. Next she worked at Niagara Falls on "The Maid of Mist", a boat for tourists. After that she worked on a farm with animals. In Toronto she didn't really work.

____/6

c) Maura met interesting people while travelling around. Write one sentence about each person
she met and something you know about them. Write in complete sentences.

First Maura met Ms Daisy, an elderly woman who works at the homeless shelter in New York City. She could live with her while she worked there. In Canada on the bridge from the USA to Canada she met Mr Tompson who has a family and a farm with animals. He has cows, pigs and hen. Later in Toronto Maura met Anne, another German girl and she stayed with her and they did lots of activities together.

____/6

II. Vocabulary

1. Give a definition for the following words. Write in complete sentences

a) editorial: *It's an important article on the first page of a newspaper.*

b) couch potato: *If you are sitting on a couch all day long, watching TV and eating unhealthy food you are a couch potato.*

c) volunteer: *A volunteer does work without getting money for it. Oftentimes the work he does is to help other people / those in need.*

d) to carry sth. out: *If someone carries something out he completes or does a task he is told to do.*

____/4

2. Translate these sentences from German to English and from English to German

a) Sie war eine Bewerberin für das Praktikum in der Anwaltskanzlei.

She was an applicant for the internship at the law firm.

b) She crossed her fingers for him.

Sie hat ihm die Daumen gedrückt.

c) Sie hat diesen Beruf gewählt, weil sie bedürfigen Menschen helfen will.

She chose this career because she wanted to help people in need.

d) I took a year off and packed my bags to meet up with my cousin in Delaware.

Ich habe mir ein Jahr frei genommen, habe meine Sachen gepackt, um mich mit meinem Cousin in Delaware zu treffen.

____/4

III. Mary's unusual hobby

In this extract from an article published in the youth magazine "pop up" you will read about Mary's unusual hobby – reading out books aloud to cheer up other people.

1. Fill in the verbs in the correct tense. You will need the progressive form once or twice

"Actually I *always wanted* (want + always) to play soccer before I *was* (be) 12", 15-year-old Mary *told* (tell) our reporter, Tom, on a sunny day in September. They *were sitting* (sit) in a nice café. Tom *has asked* (ask) Mary to come and tell him about her unusual hobby. "But as a 12-year-old girl living in a small town I *had* (have) no chance to find enough girls for our team. My second favourite hobby at that time *was* (be) reading books – and it *has now become* (become + now) my number one. I think I *have read* (read) about 500 books since I *have started* (start) reading at the age of 5. But then, I *usually did* (do + usually) it in a loud voice. I *had to become* (must + become) pretty good at it later...

____/12

2. Gerund or infinitive? Fill in the correct form. Sometimes you need to add a preposition

... I still remember *imitating* (imitate) the voices of the characters in the book. My mother used *to stop* (stop) her housework *to listen* (listen) to my words. And she encouraged me *to go on* (go on). Another step in my "career" was my little brother. He never stopped *asking* (ask) me if I could read him something. And I gave in, because I enjoyed *looking at* (look at) his big eyes.

One day my neighbour asked me if I was interested *in reading* (read) stories to children in the local hospital. I agreed *to go* (go) there once a week."

____/8

Tipps und Hinweise
Das **Gerund** wird als Substantiv, das von einem Verb abgeleitet ist, verwendet (substantiviertes Verb). Es steht nach bestimmten **Adjektiven mit Präpositionen** z.B. ***be afraid of, be worried about / be bad / good at*** ; nach bestimmten **Präpositionen** wie z.B. ***before, after***; nach bestimmten **Verben** z.B. ***enjoy, love, keep, prefer, start***; nach bestimmten **Verben mit Präposition** z.B. ***look forward to, think about, talk about*** und nach bestimmten **Nomen mit Präpositionen** z.B. ***a chance of, a way of.***

Der **Infinitiv mit to** wird nach bestimmten Verben z.B. ***decide, agree***, nach Verb + Objekt z.B. ***want***; nach Fragewörtern z.B. ***what***; nach Nomen z.B. ***place***. Außerdem steht er nach ***the first, the last, the only*** und nach der Konstruktion: **Adjektiv / Nomen + for + Nomen / Pronomen.**

3. Mary is writing in her diary. Fill in the correct verb form. Be careful with the different tenses

"Today *was* (be) such a wonderful day. I *had* (have) so much fun at the interview with Tom. He *is* (be) such a nice man. While I *was telling* (tell) him about my favourite hobby I *realized* (realize) that it really is something good. I *am* (be) able to help children and cheer them up and what is there better than *making* (make) someone smile? I think, in the future I am *going to* (read) more. I am *going to make* (make) more time for the reading. I think it *will be* (be) great.

____/10

IV. Text Production

Imagine you are writing for your school's magazine. You are supposed to write about your favourite hobby: making others happy. Write about what you do to make others happy

I love singing. I have been singing all my life I think. My mum says that I sang before I talked properly. I don't remember that of course but I do remember taking lessons and joining a choir when I was five years old. I don't only love to sing, I also love to sing for others. Sometimes I go to the hospital and sing for old people or people who are really sick. They are very happy when I sing for them. Sometimes they sing with me or ask for a specific song. During Christmas time I sometimes sing on the streets of our town. People stop by and give me some money. I donate the money to the orphanage so that the kids can have some presents on Christmas.

____ /30

Total ____/92

Tipps und Hinweise

Text Production
Before writing
- Brainstorm on the topic. Develop an opinion.
- Write down your opinion of your problem or describe the situation.
- Find facts, examples, etc. to support your opinion (e.g. in form of a mind map).
- Put in a logical order the information which you have found.
- If you are dealing with a controversial subject, think about the opposite position and find arguments to reject it.
- Find a good conclusion.

While writing
- Begin your statement with an introduction to the problem, e.g. in form of a summary of your understanding of the subject.
- Give your opinion.
- Support your opinion with the facts you have found.
- Sum up the problem and your opinion and bring your understatement to a conclusion.

After writing
- Re-read your text. Have you covered the essential points?
- Check if you have observed the rules above.
- Are your arguments convincing to someone who might not agree with you?

2. Schulaufgabe aus dem Englischen

Name: ______________________________

Stoff: Unit 2

I. Reading Comprehension

Read the following text. Pay good attention because you will have to answer questions at the end

Peter Sullivan was very excited. Next Friday was finally the week of 4th of July. It was going to be Independence Day. Peter couldn't wait for Friday. He was planning a party with all of his classmates. His parents were going to be out of town and he wanted to use this chance to invite everyone over. Peter knew that his classmates thought he was boring and this was his chance to prove them wrong. 4th of July was such an important date in the US and Peter knew that all of his classmates wanted to celebrate. He also knew that they were all still too young to drink. Peter had the key to his dad's liquor cabinet. He wasn't supposed to drink or use the alcohol because he was only fifteen. One time when his parents were out of town he got the key to the liquor cabinet remade. He promised the boys in his class that there would be drinking at his party and they all said they would come. Peter wasn't sure what to wear. He wanted to impress Solane. She was new in the class and moved last year from Costa Rica. He knew that she was single and he wanted to use the party to get to know her a little better. Maybe even more. Maybe she would kiss him. He had everything planned. First everyone would arrive. He'd have a welcome drink ready for all. Then they would have hot dogs. It was the easiest food Peter could think off and also the only he could afford. He asked his classmates to bring some candy and he was hoping they would. He also bought some chips in case anyone wanted some. After the food he would take out some more alcohol. Once Solane was tipsy he wanted to tell her that he liked her. He was hoping she'd say that she liked him too. If everyone stayed for the fireworks in the neighbourhood they should be gone by 10 p.m. the latest. That would be perfect for him to start cleaning up. His parents would come back the next morning. This way, everything would work out.

Questions on the text
Answer the following questions by ticking off the right answer

	true	false	not in text
Peter is inviting his class to a birthday party.			
Peter wants to impress the boys in his class.			
Solane moved to town last month.			
Solane moved to town from Costa Rica.			
Peter's parents know about the party.			
Peter's parents are going to a 4th of July party.			
Peter wants to eat corn dogs.			
He is going to buy chips.			
Peter likes alcohol.			
There will be alcohol at the party.			

Peter ○ stole the key to the liquor cabinet ○ had the key remade ○ is hiding the key.

Peter's parents ○ think it's ok if he drinks alcohol ○ think it's not ok if he drinks alcohol.

Solane ○ is a girl ○ is a boy.

Peter ○ is very popular in his class ○ has lots of friends ○ is a little bit boring.

Peter wants to ○ make new friends ○ impress his class ○ fall in love.

II. Vocabulary

1. Give a synonym of these words (say in other words) and the translation into German

a) to injure (in war) :_______________________ Translation: _______________________

b) a kind of: _______________________ Translation: _______________________

c) a few: _______________________ Translation: _______________________

2. Translate these sentences into English

a) Anna putzt die Badewanne im Bad und nimmt später ein Bad.

____

____

b) Franz hat mit seiner Freundin Schluss gemacht, um mit einem Model zusammen zu sein.

____

____

c) Wenn ich erwachsen bin, werde ich eine ordentliche Party veranstalten.

____

____

3. Explain these words in English. Use complete sentences

a) Sympathetic: ____

____

____

b) row: 1. ____

____

2\. ____

____

III. Grammar

1. Stressing sentence parts
Alan is planning a holiday in the USA. He's at the travel agent's
Answer the question in full sentences. Use *five different ways* of stressing the answers

1\. The travel agent: Do you need a train ticket?

Alan: No, ____

2\. The travel agent: I don't think you have a credit card?

Alan: ____

3\. The travel agent: Did your mother give you her credit card?

Alan: ____

4\. The travel agent: Do you sometimes have money problems abroad?

Alan: ____

5\. The travel agent: You must be pleased to be going on holiday soon.

Alan: ____

2. The German "lassen"

Alan is thinking about the holiday. Translate the following sentences into English using the correct constructions with let, make or have. Don't change the tenses

1. Zum Glück lassen mich meine Eltern dieses Jahr alleine in den Urlaub fahren.

____

____

2. Letztes Jahr ließ mich meine Mutter sie jeden Tag anrufen.

____

____

3. Aber dann war mein Handy kaputt, und ich ließ es reparieren.

____

____

4. Für den nächsten Urlaub werden mich meine Eltern selbst bezahlen lassen.

____

____

5. Ich muss jetzt zum Friseur (= the hairdresser) gehen. Bevor ich in den Urlaub fahre, lasse ich mir immer die Haare schneiden.

____

____

IV. Grammar

Having arrived in the USA, Alan is visiting Plimoth Plantation. He's talking to one of the actors at the living history museum
Fill in the gaps. You must find the right words for the expression in brackets
(+) agree or (–) disagree

Alan: Wow! This is like a real-life computer game. I like living history museums!

The actor: ____________________(+).

Alan: But it must take hours for the actors to ____________________ (put on their clothes). And I couldn't talk to people all day long. You know, I'm not good at telling stories.

The actor: __________________ (+). But I love my job because you needn't talk much; you simply show people what life was like in the 17th century. That's my ____________________ (the thing I aim for in life).

Alan: Hey, I don't think it was right that the colonists used ______________________________ (behaviour that is meant to hurt or kill sb.) against the British in the War of Independence.

The actor: ____________________ (–). You don't know how mean the British were after they had won the war against France. After some time the gap had become ______________________ (impossible to overcome) and the colonists fought back. But this wasn't in the 17th century. The war of Independence started only at the end of the 18th century. I would like to know eveything about the settlers!

Alan: __________________________________ (–). Sorry, but that's too much information for one day. I must go now.

The actor: ________________________________ (+). I must ___________________________ (repair) my hut.

V. Text Production

"Violent computer games make teenagers aggressive. They should be banned by law."
Do you agree or disagree? Write a comment (about 120 words)
(Use an extra sheet of paper)

Good luck !

Lösung: 2. Schulaufgabe aus dem Englischen

I. Reading Comprehension

Read the following text. Pay good attention because you will have to answer questions at the end

Peter Sullivan was very excited. Next Friday was finally the week of 4th of July. It was going to be Independence Day. Peter couldn't wait for Friday. He was planning a party with all of his classmates. His parents were going to be out of town and he wanted to use this chance to invite everyone over. Peter knew that his classmates thought he was boring and this was his chance to prove them wrong. 4th of July was such an important date in the US and Peter knew that all of his classmates wanted to celebrate. He also knew that they were all still too young to drink. Peter had the key to his dad's liquor cabinet. He wasn't supposed to drink or use the alcohol because he was only fifteen. One time when his parents were out of town he got the key to the liquor cabinet remade. He promised the boys in his class that there would be drinking at his party and they all said they would come. Peter wasn't sure what to wear. He wanted to impress Solane. She was new in the class and moved last year from Costa Rica. He knew that she was single and he wanted to use the party to get to know her a little better. Maybe even more. Maybe she would kiss him. He had everything planned. First everyone would arrive. He'd have a welcome drink ready for all. Then they would have hot dogs. It was the easiest food Peter could think off and also the only he could afford. He asked his classmates to bring some candy and he was hoping they would. He also bought some chips in case anyone wanted some. After the food he would take out some more alcohol. Once Solane was tipsy he wanted to tell her that he liked her. He was hoping she'd say that she liked him too. If everyone stayed for the fireworks in the neighbourhood they should be gone by 10 p.m. the latest. That would be perfect for him to start cleaning up. His parents would come back the next morning. This way, everything would work out.

Questions on the text

Answer the following questions by ticking off the right answer

	true	false	not in text
Peter is inviting his class to a birthday party.		*x*	
Peter wants to impress the boys in his class.		*x*	
Solane moved to town last month.		*x*	
Solane moved to town from Costa Rica.	*x*		
Peter's parents knew about the party.			*x*
Peter's parents are going to a 4th of July party.			*x*
Peter wants to eat corn dogs.		*x*	
He is going to buy chips.	*x*		
Peter likes alcohol.			*x*
There will be alcohol at the party.	*x*		

____/10

Peter ○ stole the key to the liquor cabinet ⊗ had the key remade ○ is hiding the key.

Peter's parents ○ think it's ok if he drinks alcohol ⊗ think it's not ok if he drinks alcohol.

Solane ⊗ is a girl ○ is a boy.

Peter ○ is very popular in his class ○ has lots of friends. ⊗ is a little bit boring.

Peter wants to ○ make new friends ⊗ impress his classmates ○ fall in love.

____/5

II. Vocabulary

1. Give a synonym of these words (say in other words) and the translation into German

a) to injure (in war) *to wound* Translation: *verwunden*

b) a kind of: *a sort of* Translation: *Sorte, Art*

c) a few: *a couple of, several* Translation: *einige, ein paar*

____/6

2. Translate these sentences into English

a) Anna putzt die Badewanne im Bad und nimmt später ein Bad.

Anna is cleaning the bath in the bathroom and is later taking a bath.

b) Franz hat mit seiner Freundin Schluss gemacht, um mit einem Model zusammen zu sein.

Franz dumped his girlfriend to be with a model.

c) Wenn ich erwachsen bin, werde ich eine ordentliche Party veranstalten.

When I am grown up I am going to throw a proper party. ____/6

3. Explain these words in English. Use complete sentences

a) Sympathetic: *If you are sympathetic you are very understanding with others and their feelings.*

b) row: 1. *If two people have a row with each other they are arguing / quarrelling / fighting.*

2. *A row of seats is where you can sit down for example in a theatre.*

____/3

III. Grammar

1. Stressing sentence parts
Alan is planning a holiday in the USA. He's at the travel agent's
Answer the question in full sentences. Use *five different ways* of stressing the answers

1. The travel agent: Do you need a train ticket?

Alan: No, *what I need is a plane ticket.*

2. The travel agent: I don't think you have a credit card?

Alan: *I do have a credit card.*

3. The travel agent: Did your mother give you her credit card?

Alan: *It was my father who gave me his credit card.*

4. The travel agent: Do you sometimes have money problems abroad?

Alan: *I'm always having money problems abroad.*

5. The travel agent: You must be pleased to be going on holiday soon.

Alan: *I'm really pleased to be going on holiday soon.*

____/5

Tipps und Hinweise
Hervorhebungen von Satzteilen kannst du auf verschiedene Weise machen:
- Hervorhebung mit ***do:*** du kannst hiermit spontan Gefühle ausdrücken oder eine Aufforderung unterstreichen, außerdem kannst du jemandem widersprechen.
- Hervorhebung mit ***it is / it was:*** mit it is / it was kannst du jeden Satzteil (außer Verb) hervorheben.
- Hervorhebung mit **what-Sätzen**: mit ***what*** + eine Form von ***be*** kannst du Satzteile hervorheben.
- Du kannst auch das ***present progressive*** zum Hervorheben von Verwunderung und Verärgerung benützen. (Zusätzlich zum present progressive kannst du noch das Adverb ***always*** verwenden.)
- Mit **Adverbien** kannst du auch hervorheben. Einige Beispiele sind ***really, absolutely, very, often, quite, completely, even terribly…***

2. The German "lassen"

Alan is thinking about the holiday. Translate the following sentences into English using the correct constructions with let, make or have. Don't change the tenses

1. Zum Glück lassen mich meine Eltern dieses Jahr alleine in den Urlaub fahren.

Fortunately my parents let me go on holiday alone this year.

2. Letztes Jahr ließ mich meine Mutter sie jeden Tag anrufen.

Last year my mother made me call her every day.

3. Aber dann war mein Handy kaputt, und ich ließ es reparieren.

But then my mobile was broken and I had it repaired.

4. Für den nächsten Urlaub werden mich meine Eltern selbst bezahlen lassen.

My parents will make me pay fort the next holiday myself.

5. Ich muss jetzt zum Friseur (= the hairdresser) gehen. Bevor ich in den Urlaub fahre, lasse ich mir immer die Haare schneiden.

I must go to the hairdresser's now. Before I go on holiday, I always have my hair cut.

____/10

Tipps und Hinweise
Let verwendet man, wenn man davon redet, dass man etwas zulässt, jemandem erlaubt, etwas zu tun.
Make bedeutet, dass einem jemanden dazu zwingt etwas zu tun bzw. veranlasst, dass etwas passiert.
Mit ***have + direct object + past participle*** drückt man aus, dass jemand sich etwas von jemand anderem machen lässt (z.B. Haare schneiden: *I had my hair cut.* Ich ließ mir die Haare schneiden).

IV. Grammar

Having arrived in the USA, Alan is visiting Plimoth Plantation. He's talking to one of the actors at the living history museum
Fill in the gaps. You must find the right words for the expression in brackets (+) agree or (–) disagree

Alan: Wow! This is like a real-life computer game. I like living history museums!

The actor: *So do I* (+).

Alan: But it must take hours for the actors to *get dressed* (put on their clothes). And I couldn't talk to people all day long. You know, I'm not good at telling stories.

The actor: *Nor / Neither am I* (+). But I love my job because you needn't talk much; you simply show people what life was like in the 17th century. That's my *ambition* (the thing I aim for in life).

Alan: I don't think it was right that the colonists used *violence* (behaviour that is meant to hurt or kill sb.) against the British in the War of Independence.

The actor: *But I do* (–). You don't know how mean the British were after they had won the war against France. After some time the gap had become *unbridgeable* (impossible to overcome) and the colonists fought back. But this wasn't in the 17th century. The war of Independence started only at the end of the 18th century. I would like to know everything about the settlers!

Alan: *I don't* (–). Sorry, but that's too much information for one day. I must go now.

The actor: *So must I* (+). I must *fix up* (repair) my hut.

____/10

Tipps und Hinweise:
Bejahte Kurzsätze kannst du mit ***so*** schreiben. Es steht immer das ***so*** am Satzanfang, dann folgt das ***auxiliary*** und das ***subject,*** z.B. I, you, Phil.
Verneinte Kurzsätze schreibst du mit ***nor*** und ***neither***. Im vorangegangenen Satz steht hier ein negatives ***auxiliary.*** Im Verneinungssatz ist hier auch die Satzstellung ähnlich wie beim bejahten Kurzsatz. Am Satzanfang steht ***nor*** oder ***neither,*** dann das ***auxiliary*** und dann das ***subject.***

V. Text Production

"Violent computer games make teenagers aggressive. They should be banned by law." Do you agree or disagree?

Teenagers often play violent computer games. Sometimes there are war scenes where people get shot or cruel, mean animals come and kill other animals. In a lot of the violent video games weapons are used. Since many teenagers are playing these games they are encouraged to be violent and aggressive. The characters that they want to be in the videogames are aggressive and violent, too. It is dangerous to have younger kids play those games. They get a wrong impression on violence and think it is ok to be violent and aggressive. Because of all the negative factors violent video games have the law should ban them. If teenagers weren't allowed to play them they might be softer and less aggressive.

____/30

Total ____/79

Tipps und Hinweise
Achte beim Schreiben eines Textes darauf, dass du eine kurze Einleitung gibst, die das Thema des Textes nennt. Nenne dann deine Argumente oder Fakten **für** bzw. **gegen das Thema** und komme ganz zum Schluss am Ende zu deiner **persönlichen Meinung**. Wie stehst du zu dem Thema? Bist du dafür oder dagegen?

2. Schulaufgabe aus dem Englischen

Name: ______________________________

Stoff: Unit 3 + Focus 2

I. Listening Comprehension *(Text aus Lösung 2x vorlesen lassen)*

1. Answer the following questions on the text

a) What are the professions Jack has considered working as? Give five examples and say where he would work if he did this job. (Example: astronaut: John has thought about being an astronaut. If he was an astronaut he would work in the space in a space shuttle.)

____

____

____

____

____

____

b) Why is Amy frustrated? Tell at least three reasons.

____

____

____

____

____

c) What are Jack and Amy planning on doing?

____

____

____

____

____

2. Answer the following questions by ticking off true / false or not in the text

Statement	true	false	not in text
Amy thought about being a hairdresser.			
Jack is Amy's brother.			
Amy's dad is supporting her.			
Jack and Amy are a couple.			
Amy has thought about many different jobs.			
John thought about owning a taxi company.			
John and Amy live in England.			
John and Amy are finishing school soon.			

II. Vocabulary

1. Which job suits which character?
Match each job with one of the adjectives in the right-hand column. Then write one or two sentences in English about each of the jobs. Say why you matched a certain job with a certain adjective by referring to a typical activity
Example: A teacher needs to be strict. Lazy pupils would not work, if teachers did not put pressure on them

Beruf	**Eigenschaft**
Anwalt	kreativ
Bankangestellter	sensibel
Ingenieur	gut in Mathematik
Krankenschwester	verantwortungsbewusst
Zahnarzt	ehrgeizig
Modedesigner	vertrauenswürdig

1. ____

____

2. ____

____

3. ____

____

4. ____

____

5. ____

____

6. ____

____

2. Word Power

a) Complete the text with the words in brackets! Be careful about the grammatical form

A friend of mine is quite a poor chap. He only has got 100 pounds on his ________________ (1, Sparkonto). So he cannot afford the small ______________________________________ (2, Reihenhaus) he dreams of. However, it is true that he also works a lot. He works in a ______________________ (3, Firma) which ____________________ (4, beschäftigen) 15,000 workers. He works in ____________________ (5, Vertrieb / Verkauf). Although he knows that working overtime ________________________ (6, sich auswirken auf) his health and his family life, he never manages to finish work before 8 p.m. He should try to work more ______________________ (7, effizient).

b) Use the words from a) to answer the following questions

What is the noun of word number 6: ______________________

Give a word of the same family for word

number 1: ________________________

number 5: ________________________

III. Text Production

Imagine you could do any job in the world. You could be a rockstar, a hairdresser, a doctor, a nurse… anything. Write about your dream job. Write at least five things you love about this job or reasons why you would choose it. Write two things that isn't so great about the job. Why are you perfect for the job? Write about 120 words (Use an extra sheet of paper)

Good luck !

Lösung: 1. Schulaufgabe aus dem Englischen

I. Listening Comprehension *(Text 2x vorlesen lassen)*

When Amy Miller's mum asked her what she wanted to be once she grew up Amy replied: "A lawyer". Her mother thought Amy was joking and asked her if she meant hairdresser or nurse. Amy didn't want to argue and knew that her mum didn't think she could make it to college and become successful. She went downstairs to her dad's office and asked: "Dad, do you think that I can be a lawyer some day?" Her dad replied: "Of course, Amy! You can do anything you set out to do." "Mum thought I was joking when I told her. I don't like that no one is taking me serious."

Amy met her friend Jack that afternoon and complained to him about her parents. Why didn't her mum take her serious and respect her dreams and hopes for the future. Jack was very understanding. He himself had troubles finding someone that would even consider taking his wish of being an astronaut one day serious. Jack hadn't met one single person, besides Amy, that didn't laugh when he said that. Jack had thought about other jobs. Working as a taxi driver, doctor, engineer, pilot, truck driver or pharmacist yet nothing had been interesting enough to still be in discussion.

Jack was able to comfort Amy and told her "Amy, listen, the two of us will be happy one day, you as a lawyer and I as an astronaut. And we shouldn't care so much what the world thinks. We just need to do our thing. Really, come on, we can do this. We're young, we're smart and we have dreams. Let's live them. At least, let's try." "Oh Jack, you're the best!" Amy was glad and thankful to have Jack.

1. Answer the following questions on the text

a) What are the professions Jack has considered working as? Give five examples and say where he would work if he did this job. (Example: astronaut: John has thought about being an astronaut. If he was an astronaut he would work in the space in a space shuttle.)

Jack has thought about becoming a taxi driver. He would drive around town with taxis if he did that. He has also thought about being a doctor. If he was a doctor he would work at a hospital or a private clinic. Furthermore Jack thought about becoming an engineer. He could work at a firm or local company if he was an engineer. Jack also thought about being a pharmacist. Pharmacists work at a pharmacy or laboratory. If John became a pilot he would fly airplanes or helicopters. As a truck driver John would drive trucks all over the country. He would probably work for one company.

b) Why is Amy frustrated? Tell at least three reasons.

Amy is frustrated because her mother doesn't take her serious. She is also frustrated because no one seems to think that she can become a lawyer one day. She is also frustrated because her mum doesn't believe in her.

c) What are Jack and Amy planning on doing?

Jack and Amy are planning on following their dreams and becoming an astronaut and a lawyer. They think that they can achieve these goals and believe in themselves and each other.

____/10

2. Answer the following questions by ticking off true / false or not in the text

	true	false	not in text
Amy thought about being a hairdresser.		*x*	
Jack is Amy's brother.		*x*	
Amy's dad is supporting her.	*x*		
Jack and Amy are a couple.			*x*
Amy has thought about many different jobs.		*x*	
John thought about owning a taxi company.		*x*	
John and Amy live in England.			*x*
John and Amy are finishing school soon.			*x*

____/8

II. Vocabulary

1. Which job suits which character?
Match each job with one of the adjectives in the right-hand column. Then write one or two sentences in English about each of the jobs. Say why you matched a certain job with a certain adjective by referring to a typical activity
Example: A teacher needs to be strict. Lazy pupils would not work, if teachers did not put pressure on them

Beruf	**Eigenschaft**
Anwalt	kreativ
Bankangestellter	sensibel
Ingenieur	gut in Mathematik
Krankenschwester	verantwortungsbewusst
Zahnarzt	ehrgeizig
Modedesigner	vertrauenswürdig

1. *An engineer must be good at maths because he has to know technical things.*
2. *A nurse should be trust-worthy so that her patients can tell her their sorrows.*
3. *A fashion designer must be creative so that he can imagine new styles.*
4. *A lawyer should be ambitious so that he gets more money with his growing skills.*
5. *A dentist must be sensitive so that he doesn't hurt his patients during the treatment.*
6. *A bank accountant should be responsible so that people are not worried about their money.*

____/24

2. Word power

a) Complete the text with the words in brackets! Be careful about the grammatical form!

A friend of mine is quite a poor chap. He only has got 100 pounds on his *savings account* (1, Sparkonto). So he cannot afford the small *terraced house* (2, Reihenhaus) he dreams of. However, it is true that he also works a lot. He works in a *firm* (3, Firma) which *employs* (4, beschäftigen) 15,000 workers. He works in *sales department* (5, Vertrieb / Verkauf). Although he knows that working overtime *affects* (6, sich auswirken auf) his health and his family life, he never manages to finish work before 8 p.m. He should try to work more *efficient* (7, effizient).

b) Use the words from a) to answer the following questions!

What is the noun of word number 6: *an effect = Auswirkung*

Give a word of the same family for word

number 1: *savings = Ersparnis*

number 5: *to sell sth. to sb. = jmd. etw. verkaufen*

____/10

III. Text Production

Imagine you could do any job in the world. You could be a rockstar, a hairdresser, a doctor, a nurse… anything. Write about your dream job. Write at least five things you love about this job or reasons why you would choose it. Write two things that isn't so great about the job. Why are you perfect for the job?

If I could do any job in the world I would chose to be a kids nurse. First of all I love to be with children. Nurses help people and in this case kids and I think it's a great way to help. I like that you can make children smile and play with them and take care of them. I would like that I am able to learn a lot about different diseases. I think it is great to work in a team and as a nurse you work in a team with the doctors, the other nurses and the patients. Negative effects could be the hard work and working at Christmas or other holidays. I think I would be perfect for the job because I love kids and helping others.

____/ 30

Total ____/82

Tipps und Hinweise

Text Production
Before writing
- Brainstorm on the topic. Develop an opinion.
- Write down your opinion of your problem or describe the situation.
- Find facts, examples, etc. to support your opinion (e.g. in form of a mind map).
- Put in a logical order the information which you have found.
- If you are dealing with a contoversial subject, think about the opposite position and find arguments to reject it.
- Find a good conclusion.

While writing
- Begin your statement with an introduction to the problem, e.g. in form of a summary of your understanding of the subject.
- Give your opinion.
- Support your opinion with the facts you have found.
- Sum up the problem and your opinion and bring your understatement to a conclusion.

After writing
- Re-read your text. Have you covered the essential points?
- Check if you have observed the rules above.
- Are your arguments convincing to someone who might not agree with you?

3. Schulaufgabe aus dem Englischen

Name: ___________________________

Stoff: Unit 4–5

I. Reading Comprehension

Read the following text. Answer the questions afterwards

When the states west of Mississippi weren't yet part of the today called United States of America, those states were known as the "Wild West". Mostly Angloamericans and some European immigrants started to settle in and urbanize those areas. In 1890 these areas became part of the United States. Some of the clichés of the Wild West are freedom, the right of the more powerful, and fighting for ones possessions. In the early 19th century people started to write magazines about the so-called Wild West. There were novels about "Buffalo Bill" in the 1870. Buffalo Bill, whose real name William Frederic Cody came up with the idea of having a Wild West show, because of the popularity of those books and magazines. He was hoping the show would be as successful and it was. The Buffalo Bill show went on international tourneys and was known in many places.
There was also a boom in the film industry. Wild Western films are up to this day a great attraction.
"Into the West" a film by Steven Spielberg tells the story of an Angloamerican and his wife. It plays between 1827 and 1890. The film which consists six parts, is trying to give details of the Wild Western time. Karl May tried to bring the Wild West to Germany in his novels. Winnetou is one example for it. Lucy Luke is another example of how the Wild West is portrayed in Europe.

Statement	**true**	**false**	**not in text**
Buffalo Bill is an Angloamerican.			
Buffalo Bill is a Wild Western show.			
William Frederic Cody lived in the 18th century.			
Some of the clichés of the Wild West were poverty and freedom.			
"Into the Wild" is a film by Steven Spielberg.			
Buffalo Bill wrote novels.			
There were only black people in the Wild West.			
There were only white people in the Wild West.			
Wild Western films are known today.			
The Wild West took place in the 18th century.			

II. Vocabulary

Explain the following words in English. Write complete sentences

a) entire: ____

____

b) to struggle: ____

____

c) to occur to sb.:____

____

d) tame: ____

____

e) unemployment: ____

____

f) to regain: ____

____

g) to gather: ____

____

h) greed: ____

____

i) to be in charge of sth.: ____

____

j) to praise: ____

____

k) biased: ____

____

l) to shiver: ____

____

m) to weep: ____

____

n) to embrace: ____

____

III. Grammar

1. Write a text using the following words in their given order. Write 14–16 sentences (= one word in each sentences). The text must be coherent (= zusammenhängend) Make sure that your tenses make sense

was walking, saw, shot, didn't show, would never have gone, thought, cutting, had made, wanted, to prepare, looking, met, surprised, not knowing, ran

____

____

____

____

____

____

____

____

____

2. Fill in the blanks by using the words in the box. Be careful to use the right participles and participle constructions of those words

to have * to ignore * to complain * to insult * to live * to remember * to ask * to know

Sir, ____________________ next to a family with children ____________________ massive problems, we have become worried about the way some parents treat their children. Often ____________________ the questions ____________________ by their children, parents don't have proper conversations with them. The ____________________ thing is that a number of adults ____________________ by their children even beat them, ____________________ that they themselves were once beaten by their parents. Although ____________________ that it does not really help, they say that beating violent children is necessary. ____________________ about children insisting on doing what they want, adults should sometimes think about their own responsibility.

Yours sincerely,

Susan

IV. Mediation

Read the following German text. Write a short summary afterwards (in English)
Write complete sentences and between 80–100 words

Der „vierte Juli“ ist auch als der Geburtstag der Vereinigten Staaten von Amerika bekannt. An diesem Feiertag feiern die Amerikaner die Unterzeichnung der Unabhängigkeitserklärung vom 4. Juli 1776. Damals gab es in Amerika 13 Kolonien, die alle an der Ostküste Amerikas lagen. Die Unabhängigkeitserklärung wurde von allen Anführern der 13 Kolonien unterschrieben. Somit waren die Vereinigten Staaten von Amerika gegründet.

Bis heute wird der 4. Juli groß gefeiert. Die Amerikaner veranstalten Feuerwerke, Umzüge, ziehen sich in blau-weiß-rot an. Die Fahne wird aufgehängt, die Nachbarn werden eingeladen und man grillt zusammen und feiert sein Land. In größeren Städten gibt es auch größere Feste und bei allen viel Freude. Überall sieht man bunte Fahnen auf die Gesichter gemalt, alle sind stolz Amerikaner zu sein. In New York City gibt es jedes Jahr ein großes Feuerwerk zum Geburtstag und alle New Yorker versammeln sich am Hudson River, um das Spektakel mitzuerleben. Kein Land feiert seinen Geburtstag wie Amerika – bunt, froh und viel.

Good luck !

Lösung: 3. Schulaufgabe aus dem Englischen

I. Reading Comprehension

Read the following text. Answer the questions afterwards.

When the states west of Mississippi weren't yet part of the today called United States of America, those states were known as the "Wild West". Mostly Angloamericans and some European immigrants started to settle in and urbanize those areas. In 1890 these areas became part of the United States. Some of the clichés of the Wild West are freedom, the right of the more powerful, and fighting for ones possessions. In the early 19th century people started to write magazines about the so-called Wild West. There were novels about "Buffalo Bill" in the 1870. Buffalo Bill, whose real name William Frederic Cody came up with the idea of having a Wild West show, because of the popularity of those books and magazines. He was hoping the show would be as successful and it was. The Buffalo Bill show went on international tourneys and was known in many places.

There was also a boom in the film industry. Wild Western films are up to this day a great attraction.

"Into the West" a film by Steven Spielberg tells the story of an Angloamerican and his wife. It plays between 1827 and 1890. The film which consists six parts, is trying to give details of the Wild Western time. Karl May tried to bring the Wild West to Germany in his novels. Winnetou is one example for it. Lucy Luke is another example of how the Wild West is portrayed in Europe.

Statement	**true**	**false**	**not in text**
Buffalo Bill is an Angloamerican.		*x*	
Buffalo Bill is a Wild Western show.	*x*		
William Frederic Cody lived in the 18th century.		*x*	
Some of the clichés of the Wild West were poverty and freedom.		*x*	
"Into the Wild" is a film by Steven Spielberg.		*x*	
Buffalo Bill wrote novels.	*x*		
There were only black people in the Wild West.			*x*
There were only white people in the Wild West.			*x*
Wild Western films are known today.	*x*		
The Wild West took place in the 18th century.		*x*	

____/10

II. Vocabulary

Explain the following words in English. Write complete sentences

a) entire: *The entire thing means the whole thing, all of it.*

b) to struggle: *If you struggle with something you are having a hard time with it.*

c) to occur to sb.: *If something occurs to you it comes to your mind.*

d) tame: *An animal that is tame is very calm and easy to handle.*

e) unemployment: *Unemployment is a state when you don't have a job.*

f) to regain: *To regain something means to get something back.*

g) to gather: *If you gather something e.g. your things you collect them together.*

h) greed: *Greed is a state in which you want more and more even if you might already have enough.*

i) to be in charge of sth.: *If you are in charge of something, you are responsible for it and it's organization.*

j) to praise: *If you praise something or someone you say something good or how great it / he is.*

k) biased: *If you have a biased opinion, you are only looking at one side and not considering the other.*

l) to shiver: *If someone shivers they are very cold and shaking a little bit.*

m) to weep: *If you weep you cry. Weep is a more formal word than cry.*

n) to embrace: *If you embrace someone you are putting your arms around him / her.*

____/14

III. Grammar

1. Write a text using the following words in their given order. Write 14–16 sentences (= one word in each sentences). The text must be coherent (= zusammenhängend) Make sure that your tenses make sense

was walking, saw, shot, didn't show, would never have gone, thought, cutting, had made, wanted, to prepare, looking, met, surprised, not knowing, ran

Mr Stup was walking in the forest when he suddenly saw someone hunting animals. He was surprised when he heard a shot. His map didn't show that hunting was allowed in this forest. If he had known this he would never have gone to this part of town. Mr Stup thought about what to do. He wasn't sure if cutting through the woods was the best idea. He had made it almost halfway through the forest yet he didn't know if this was safe any longer. He wanted to go home. He wanted to prepare dinner and eat with his wife. He was looking around trying to find the man. He saw him and their eyes met. Mr Strup was surprised at the weird expression on the man's face. Not knowing who that man was and being scared he started running. He ran all the way back to his car and was happy once he was able to drive off.

____/15

2. Fill in the blanks by using the words in the box. Be careful to use the right participles and participle constructions of those words

to have * to ignore * to complain * to insult * to live * to remember * to ask * to know

Sir, *living* next to a family with children *having* massive problems, we have become worried about the way some parents treat their children. Often *ignoring* the questions *asked* by their children, parents don't have proper conversations with them. The *surprising* thing is that a number of adults *insulted* by their children even beat them, *remembering* that they themselves were once beaten by their parents. *Although knowing* that it does not really help, they say that beating violent children is necessary. *Complaining* about children insisting on doing what they want, adults should sometimes think about their own responsibility.

Yours sincerely,

Susan ____/10

[Punktabzug bei nicht / falsch erkannten *participle constructions* und Auslassungen/Rechtschreibfehlern]

IV. Mediation

Read the following German text. Write a short summary afterwards (in English). Write complete sentences and between 80 – 100 words.

Der „vierte Juli" ist auch als der Geburtstag der Vereinigten Staaten von Amerika bekannt. An diesem Feiertag feiern die Amerikaner die Unterzeichnung der Unabhängigkeitserklärung vom 4. Juli 1776. Damals gab es in Amerika 13 Kolonien, die alle an der Ostküste Amerikas lagen. Die Unabhängigkeitserklärung wurde von allen Anführern der 13 Kolonien unterschrieben. Somit waren die Vereinigten Staaten von Amerika gegründet.

Bis heute wird der 4. Juli groß gefeiert. Die Amerikaner veranstalten Feuerwerke, Umzüge, ziehen sich in blau-weiß-rot an. Die Fahne wird aufgehängt, die Nachbarn werden eingeladen und man grillt zusammen und feiert sein Land. In größeren Städten gibt es auch größere Feste und bei allen viel Freude. Überall sieht man bunte Fahnen auf die Gesichter gemalt, alle sind stolz Amerikaner zu sein. In New York City gibt es jedes Jahr ein großes Feuerwerk zum Geburtstag und alle New Yorker versammeln sich am Hudson River um das Spektakel mitzuerleben. Kein Land feiert seinen Geburtstag wie Amerika – bunt, froh und viel.

4th of July in the United States of America

In 1776 the 13 colonies that existed in today's United States of America signed a document the so-called Declaration of Independence. This was on the 4th of July. Ever since, the United States celebrate their "birthday" on this day. It is a national holiday and everyone is celebrating together. There are fireworks, parades, parties and lot's of other things. Americans meet up with their neighbours and have barbecues to celebrate their country. They all wear blue red and white and are proud to call themselves Americans.

[4 BE Inhalt + 6 BE Sprache (Sprachrichtigkeit und Ausdrucksvermögen) mal 3 = 30 BE]

___/ 30
Total ____/79

3. Schulaufgabe aus dem Englischen

Name: ______________________________

Stoff: Unit 4–5

I. Listening Comprehension *(Text aus Lösung 2x vorlesen lassen)*

Listen to the following text twice. Answer the questions afterwards
California – the Golden State

1. Answer the following questions in complete sentences

a) Where does Anna want to go for sure once she and Max are in California?

____

____

____

____

b) What are Max' top three things or places to visit in Golden State – California?

____

____

____

____

c) Do the two of them agree somehow in their choices of where they want to go?

____

____

____

____

2. Answer the following questions by ticking off the right answer

Statement	**true**	**false**	**not in text**
Anna likes National Parks.			
Max doesn't want that Anna goes shopping.			
Anna wants to go to the beach.			
They both like nature.			
Max is going to go shopping with Anna.			
California has two active volcanoes.			

The air in California is polluted.			
Anna is interested in electronics.			
Anna and Max have already booked their flights.			
Anna's uncle Joe is going to travel with them.			
They both want to meet Hollywood stars.			
California is also known as "The sunshine State"			

II. Vocabulary

Facts about California

Give a definition for the following words. Write complete sentences

a) urban: ____

____

b) desert: ____

____

c) Mount Whitney: ____

____

d) diary: ____

____

e) agriculture: ____

____

f) to restore: ____

____

g) hazard: ____

____

h) to pollute: ____

____

i) earthquakes: ____

____

j) hydropower: ____

____

III. Grammar

Participle constructions: Shorten the following sentences by using participle constructions. If it isn't possible to use a participle, explain it in a single sentence

a) The plane that arrives from Los Angeles is late today.

____

____

b) Since (= da) Chris and Alison aren't a couple, they sleep in different rooms.

____

____

c) The woman whose car had been damaged in an accident is ...

____

____

d) After the policemen had arrived, they started arresting the hooligans.

____

____

e) The person that was found in the cellar had been kidnapped by two men.

____

____

f) Before Harry left the house, the telephone had started ringing.

____

____

g) As the Millers aren't very rich, they only can afford a very small flat.

____

____

h) After the children had cleaned the beaches, they went back to the house.

____

____

III. Translation

Nachdem Diana den Brief vom National Trust erhalten hatte, lief sie so schnell wie möglich zu Rob, um ihm die Neuigkeit zu erzählen. Leider war Rob nicht in der Arbeit. Der Mann, der im Laden arbeitete, erzählte ihr, dass er vom Besitzer zur Bank geschickt worden sei, um etwas Geld zu wechseln. Da die Bank sehr nah war, wartete Diana auf ihn.
Da Rob an dem Arbeitsurlaub nicht teilnehmen wollte, war Diana sehr enttäuscht. Nachdem sie das gehört hatte, ging sie nach Hause und wollte Rob nicht mehr sehen. Als Diana dort ankam, bemerkte sie, dass sie ihren Hausschlüssel verloren hatte. So konnte sie die Haustür nicht öffnen.

(Use an extra sheet of paper)

Good luck !

Lösung: 3. Schulaufgabe aus dem Englischen

I. Listening Comprehension *(Text 2x vorlesen lassen)*

Listen to the following text twice. Answer the questions afterwards

California – the Golden State

Anna and Max are planning their holiday in California. They are thinking about where they want to go and what they want to see. Anna loves big cities. She wants to go to Los Angeles and San Francisco. She is excited to go shopping there. Anna also wants to swim in the ocean. Santa Barbara and Santa Monica have great beaches. Those would be places Anna would like to go to. Max on the other hand isn't interested in shopping at all. He would rather go to Silicon Valley once Anna does her shopping in San Francisco. He is very interested in anything that has to do with electronic equipment and wants to be a disc jockey one day. Besides being interested in electronics, Max is also a nature person. He already read a lot about California's beautiful landscapes with its wonderful wilderness and national parks. He is determined about going to Yosemite National Park one of the most beautiful parks in Northern America. Max also wants to see Lassen Park, California's active volcano. He has never seen a volcano before and is super excited that this might be his first time.
Both Anna and Max want to go to Hollywood. They hope to see their favourite movie stars: Cameron Diaz and Brad Pitt. Both of them also want to go to the Six Flag Rollercoaster Park. They've been dreaming about riding all the roller coasters. Anna is a little frightened of the heights but still very excited.
Now the two of them just have to plan how their itinerary[1] will be. Once they are done they want to book their flights. Anna and Max's parents are very supportive of their kids. They think it is a great opportunity to go to the United States and improve their English. Max's uncle Joe lives in California and will be travelling with them the entire time so the two of them are not alone in California, the Golden State.

1. Answer the following questions in complete sentences

a) Where does Anna want to go for sure once she and Max are in California?

Anna wants to go to big cities like Los Angeles or San Fransisco to do shopping there. She also wants to go to Santa Monica and Santa Barbara to go to the beach to swim in the ocean.

b) What are Max' top three things or places to visit in Golden State – California?

Max is determined about going to Silicon Valley and the Yosemite National Park. He also wants go to Lassen Park, California's active volcano.

c) Do the two of them agree somehow in their choices of where they want to go?

Although Anna and Max do have different interests and want to see different things while they are in California they also agree on some choices. For example both of them want to go to

Hollywood to see their favourite movie stars. They also both want to go to the Six Flag Rollercoaster Park to try out the roller coasters there.

____/15

2. Answer the following questions by ticking off the right answer

	true	false	not in text
Anna likes National Parks.			*x*
Max doesn't want that Anna goes shopping.			*x*
Anna wants to go to the beach.	*x*		
They both like nature.			*x*
Max is going to go shopping with Anna.		*x*	
California has two active volcanoes.			x
The air in California is polluted.			*x*
Anna is interested in electronics.		*x*	
Anna and Max have already booked their flights.		*x*	
Anna's uncle Joe is going to travel with them.		*x*	
They both want to meet Hollywood stars.	*x*		
California is also known as "The sunshine State"			*x*

____/12

II. Vocabulary

Facts about California
Give a definition for the following words. Write complete sentences

a) urban: *A city or a town is an urban area.*

b) desert: *In a desert there is mostly sand. It is oftentimes very hot and water is rare.*

c) Mount Whitney: *Mount Whitney is the highest mountain in the USA (without Alaska) and is located in California..*

d) diary: *A journal or book in which one writes each day to remember the happenings of that day.*

e) agriculture: *The practice of farming or having animals or other crops.*

f) to restore: *If you restore something you bring / make it back into it's original state.*

g) hazard: *A hazard is a danger or risk that might belong to a special situation or sometimes a specific job.*

h) to pollute: *Polluted air is air that is dirty for example through factory smoke.*

i) earthquakes: *If the earth shakes and sometimes things or houses break there is an earthquake.*

j) hydropower: *Hydropower is the power we can get from water.*

____/10

II. Grammar

Participle constructions: Shorten the following sentences by using participle constructions. If it isn't possible to use a participle, explain it in a single sentence

a) The plane that arrives from Los Angeles is late today.

The plane arriving from Los Angeles is late today.

b) Since (= da) Chris and Alison aren't a couple, they sleep in different rooms.

Since not being a couple Chris and Alison sleep in different rooms.

c) The woman whose car had been damaged in an accident is ...

((It isn't possible to use a participle construction because there are two different subjects.))

d) After the policemen had arrived, they started arresting the hooligans.

After arriving the policemen started arresting the hooligans.

e) The person that was found in the cellar had been kidnapped by two men.

The person found in the cellar had been kidnapped by two men.

f) Before Harry left the house, the telephone had started ringing.

((It isn't possible to use a participle construction because there are two different subjects.))

g) As the Millers aren't very rich, they only can afford a very small flat.

Not being very rich the Millers only can afford a very small flat.

h) After the children had cleaned the beaches, they went back to the house.

Having cleaned the beaches the children went back to the house. ____/16

III. Translation

Nachdem Diana den Brief vom National Trust erhalten hatte, lief sie so schnell wie möglich zu Rob, um ihm die Neuigkeit zu erzählen. Leider war Rob nicht in der Arbeit. Der Mann, der im Laden arbeitete, erzählte ihr, dass er vom Besitzer zur Bank geschickt worden sei, um etwas Geld zu wechseln. Da die Bank sehr nah war, wartete Diana auf ihn.

Da Rob an dem Arbeitsurlaub nicht teilnehmen wollte, war Diana sehr enttäuscht. Nachdem sie das gehört hatte, ging sie nach Hause und wollte Rob nicht mehr sehen. Als Diana dort ankam, bemerkte sie, dass sie ihren Hausschlüssel verloren hatte. Deswegen konnte sie die Haustür nicht öffnen.

Having received the letter from National Trust Diana ran to Rob as quickly as possible to tell him the news. Unfortunately Rob wasn't at work. The man working in the shop told her that he had been sent to the bank by the counter to change some money. As the bank was very close Diana waited for him.

As Rob didn't want to take part in the working holiday Diana was very disappointed. Having heard that, she went home and didn't want to see Rob anymore. After arriving there Diana noticed that she had lost the key of her house. Therefore she wasn't able to open the door.

____/20

Total ____/73

Tipps und Hinweise

1. How to use the participle? The present participle has an ***active*** meaning, the past participle a ***passive*** meaning, z.B. the *rising* sun (to rise); *dyed* hair (to dye); the *dying* swan (to die); an *exciting* story (to excite); *annoying* adults (to annoy = *they annoy you*, d.h. *they make you feel that way*; annoyed adults (to annoy = *they are annoyed by you*, d.h. *they feel that way about you)*. 2. ***The participle can be modified by an adjective or an adverb or by a noun***, z.B. a good-looking boy, a hard-working student, a well-written story, freshly-washed clothes, an organically-grown fruit, half-finished homework, a Turkish-speaking policeman.

3. Participles used to shorten relative clauses: The boy who was standing behind the counter stole two CDs. The boy *standing* behind the counter stole two CDs. The policeman who questions young offenders have special psychological training.The policeman *questioning* young offenders have special psychological training.

4. The present participle (or infinitive) after verbs of perception. The present participle expresses an action that was / is in progress all the time while you are / were watching / listening. In a sentence without verb of perception, the verb would be in the progressive form. *The leaves were falling.* (I saw that.) *I saw the leaves falling.* The infinitive expresses an action that began and finished while you were watching. In a sentence without verb of perception the verb would be in the simple form. *He came out and left.* (I saw that.) *I saw him come out and leave.*

If you aren't sure, try the following questions: Would you say "The birds were singing. I heard that." (I heard the birds singing) or "The bird sang. I heard that." (I heard the birds sing).

Monika und Claus Arndt aus Waldtrudering geben im Eigenverlag Lernhilfen für Schüler heraus

Die Durchblick-Garanten

Die Tage sind gezählt bis zu den Sommerferien. Nicht alle Schüler jedoch tun sechs Wochen lang nichts für die Schule. Und es gibt so einige Eltern, die sich jetzt schon fürs neue Schuljahr rüsten. Viele von ihnen landen bei Monika und Claus Arndt aus Waldtrudering. Das Ehepaar gibt Hefte mit Schulproben für Grundschüler und Schulaufgaben für Gymnasiasten und Realschüler heraus. Kinder und Jugendliche können sich mit ihren Durchblicker-Aufgaben auf Prüfungen vorbereiten.

Monika und Claus Arndt im Keller ihres Waldtruderinger Hauses. Dort drucken sie ihre Durchblicker-Schulaufgaben. Jahrelang haben sie zudem Nachhilfeunterricht gegeben, mittlerweile konzentrieren sie sich auf ihr Verlagsgeschäft. Ihre Schulaufgaben sind im Buchhandel zu finden und helfen Schülern bei der Lösung von Schulaufgaben. ***Fotos: Panthermedia/ve/kn***

Im Keller der Familie Arndt im Birkhahnweg in Waldtrudering läuft der Drucker. In den Regalen stapeln sich ordentlich die Ausdrucke. Ihre Bestellungen erreichen Monika und Claus Arndt meist spät abends. Nach Ladenschluss schicken Buchhändler noch ihre Bestellliste ab, so auch an den Durchblicker Verlag in Waldtrudering. Viele Jahre lang haben die Arndts im Keller Schülern Nachhilfeunterricht gegeben. Vor fünf Jahren haben sie einen Verlag gegründet und verkaufen seitdem Bücher mit typischen Schulaufgaben für bayerische Schüler. Derzeit, kurz vor den Sommerferien und vor allem dann im September, sei die Nachfrage besonders groß. „Wir haben ein saisonales Geschäft", sagt Claus Arndt schmunzelnd. Bevor es in die Ferien geht oder zum Start ins neue Schuljahr, bestellen Schüler und ihre Eltern die Durchblicker-Schulaufgaben.

Der Mathematiker sattelte aufs Lehramt um

Die Arndts haben sozusagen eine Marktlücke entdeckt: Verlage bieten zwar immer mehr Lernhilfen für Schüler an. Doch die Arndts haben ihre Ausgaben auf die jeweiligen Schultypen und auf die neuen Lehrpläne in Bayern zugeschnitten. So läuft und läuft ihr Drucker. „Volltreffer!", hat ihnen ein Schüler geschrieben, „drei Aufgaben in meiner Schulaufgabe waren genau wie die aus Ihrem Buch!" Und eine Buchhändlerin lässt sie wissen: „Ich empfehle die Reihe immer weiter. Sie haben in mir einen Fan gefunden."
Wie aber kommt es, dass die beiden Waldtruderinger so einen guten Riecher haben, wie Lehrer ihre Schulaufgaben gestalten und was sie wollen? Claus Arndt war als Diplom-Mathematiker in der EDV-Branche beschäftigt. Bis 2004. Da hieß es: „Wer gehen wolle, könne gehen." Der Waldtruderinger Vater zweier Söhne ließ sich das nicht zwei Mal sagen. Händeringend wurde damals nach Lehrern gesucht. So sattelte der Mathematiker kurzerhand um und unterrichtete fortan an der Realschule in Dachau und am Neuperlacher Heinrich-Heine-Gymnasium Mathe.
Damit nicht genug. Zuhause im Keller eröffnete er mit seiner Frau Monika ein Lernstudio für Schüler. Claus Arndt gab Nachhilfe in Mathematik. Seine Frau in Englisch, Deutsch und Französisch. „Für Physik und Latein beschäftigten wir noch weitere Nachhilfelehrer", erzählt Claus Arndt. Die Waldtruderinger Familien nahmen das Angebot gerne an: Bei den Arndts gab es Nachhilfe für den Achtklässler, der darum kämpfte, wegen Mathe bloß nicht durchzufallen. Ein anderer Bub, ein Grundschüler, konnte partout nicht stillsitzen. „Ich ließ ihn hier unten auf einem kleinen Trampolin auf- und abspringen und fragte ihn dabei das Einmaleins ab", erzählt Claus Arndt. Ebenso ackerten gleich mehrere Schüler in einem Crashkurs, um in ihrer Abschlussprüfung eine bessere Note zu bekommen.

Nachhilfeunterricht von 13 bis 20 Uhr

Vier Jahre lang büffelten die Nachhilfelehrer mit ihren Schützlingen Stunde für Stunde im Keller. „Unseren Höhepunkt hatten wir im Jahr 2008, da saßen wir von 13 bis 20 Uhr in unserem Lernstudio, die Nachfrage in Waldtrudering und Umgebung war einfach so groß", erinnert sich Claus Arndt. Was ist das Arndtsche Erfolgsrezept? Die Arndts lösen mit ihren Schülern Schulaufgaben, erarbeiten Musterlösungen und korrigieren die Antworten gemeinsam. „Diese Klassenarbeiten denken wir uns selbst aus", sagt Claus Arndt. Im Laufe der Jahre haben sie ein Gespür dafür entwickelt, welche Aufgabentypen drankommen können — „wie die Lehrer ticken".
Schulaufgaben zu entwickeln, das machte Claus Arndt bald nicht nur für seine Nachhilfeschüler im Münchner Osten. Für die Verlage Klett und Cornelsen modifizierte er Schulaufgaben. „Doch die Lehrpläne variieren von Bundesland zu Bundesland", erzählt der Klausuren-Profi. Und so schlug man ihm vor, für Bayern einfach selbst Schulaufgaben herauszugeben. Im Eigenverlag.
Claus Arndt hatte ja mit seiner Frau Monika kompetente Hilfe an seiner Seite. Denn vor allem sie war es, die in ganz Bayern Buchhändler abklapperte, um Werbung für die Durchblicker-Schulaufgaben zu machen. Mehr noch: Monika Arndt hatte als Autorin bereits Ernährungsbücher für Kinder veröffentlicht, hatte unter anderem beim Stark-Verlag über Produktion sowie Inhalt von Lernhilfen viele Erfahrungen gesammelt und als Lektorin gearbeitet. Sie knöpfte sich nun die Fächer Deutsch, Französisch und Englisch vor und arbeitete ebenso Schulaufgaben aus. Zudem sei es für sie als Schulaufgaben-Entwickler mit Einführung des G8 leichter geworden: „Alles ist systematischer und strukturierter, ich kann eher abschätzen, was in einer Klassenarbeit drankommt", sagt Claus Arndt.

Neu im Angebot sind Proben für Grundschüler

Mittlerweile haben sie eine breite Palette mit 57 verschiedenen Ausgaben im Angebot: Ob für Gymnasiasten Mathe-Schulaufgaben von der fünften bis hoch zur zwölften Klasse oder für Realschüler Englisch-Schulaufgaben. „Und neu und sehr beliebt sind unsere Schulproben in Mathe, Deutsch und HSU für Dritt- und Viertklässler", sagt Monika Arndt. „Die sind immer mehr unsere Renner!" Als Verlag profitieren sie von dem wachsendem Druck, der schon auf Grundschüler ausgeübt werde. „Eltern wollen unbedingt, dass ihr Kind einen Notendurchschnitt von 2,33 beim Übertrittszeugnis in der vierten Klasse hat, damit es aufs Gymnasium gehen kann", sagt Claus Arndt. „Das ist oft zu viel des Guten." Er weiß, wovon er spricht. Er hat in all den Jahren in seinem Lernstudio viele Kinder kennengelernt. „Oft haben wir gemerkt, welch großen Druck Eltern auf ihr Kind ausüben können." Natürlich müsse sich jedes Kind auf Tests in der Schule vorbereiten. Doch als Eltern zweier Söhne, 1993 und 1996 geboren, wissen sie eben auch, dass ein Kind nicht zu viel lernen dürfe. „Wer für eine Schulaufgabe mit zwei unserer Aufgaben übt, dem reicht das meist", behauptet Monika Arndt.
Den beiden Schulaufgaben- und Nachhilfe-Profis geht es vor allem darum, Schüler besser auf das vorzubereiten, was sie bei einer Probe erwartet. „Angst und Nervosität legen sich schnell, wenn Schüler ähnliche Aufgaben kennen und bereits bearbeitet haben", sagt Claus Arndt.

Verena Rudolf

Telefon (089) 53 06-420
lokales@merkur.de
Telefax: (089) 53 06-86 56

Mehr Durchblick für Schüler

Claus und Monika Arndt produzieren Lernhefte im heimischen Keller in Waldtrudering

VON LAURA MÜLLER

Vielen Kindern graut es vor der Schule. Häufig sind sie unmotiviert und wissen nicht, wie sie sich auf Tests und Schularbeiten vorbereiten sollen. Für diese Problematik gibt es eine Menge Nachhilfelehrer und Bücher, die helfen sollen. Einer der Verlage, die solche Bücher, oder vielmehr Hefte, produzieren, ist der Durchblicker Verlag – ein kleiner Buchverlag, der nur aus dem Ehepaar Claus und Monika Arndt besteht. Er hat sich auf Schulaufgaben und ihre Lösungen spezialisiert. Die Arndts produzieren die Hefte im heimischen Keller in Waldtrudering.

Auf den jungen Schülern lastet eine Menge Druck, sagen die Arndts

Claus Arndt, ein ehemaliger Software-Ingenieur, hat den Verlag vor fünf Jahren gegründet. Angefangen hat alles damit, dass Claus Arndt anfing, Nachhilfe zu geben. „Als die Kinder kamen, wollte ich nicht ständig unterwegs sein", erzählte er. „Also habe ich meinen Job gekündigt und Nachhilfe gegeben." Die Schüler kamen gerne zu Claus Arndt, so wurde die Nachfrage irgendwann zu groß. Die Arndts gaben das Lernbüro auf und fingen an, Bücher mit Schulaufgaben und ihren Lösungen zu drucken. Zunächst verkauften sie nur wenige Hefte, doch im vergangenen Jahr waren es schon 20 000. Insgesamt haben sie 58 Bücher verfasst und herausgebracht. Die Arndts sehen sich mittlerweile als „ernst zu nehmende Konkurrenz" für den renommierten Stark-Verlag. Dessen rote Übungsbücher stehen bei vielen Schülern im Regal.

Claus Arndt sammelt seit der Umstellung auf das G8 Schulaufgaben von verschiedenen Schulen. Weil er selbst mal als Lehrer arbeitete, weiß er, was andere Lehrer erwarten. Claus und Monika Arndt orientieren sich bei ihren Aufgaben immer an dem neusten Stand der Lehrpläne.

Als die Arndts ihren Verlag gründeten, klapperten sie alle möglichen Büchereien ab, um ihre Bücher präsentieren zu können. Monika Arndt hat schon vorher als Lektorin und Autorin gearbeitet. Sie kennt sich in der Branche aus und weiß, wie man hier etwas erreicht. Heute liegen die Bücher des Durchblicker-Verlags etwa in Hugendubel- und Thalia-Filialen aus. „Wir freuen uns, dass unsere Bücher so gut ankommen", sagt Claus Arndt. Am besten verkaufen sich laut den Arndts die Lerntrainer für die Grundschule sowie für die 5. und 6. Klasse Gymnasium. Das verwundert. Claus Arndt erklärt: „Auf den jungen Schülern lastet schon eine Menge Druck."

Die Nachfrage ist groß: Im Keller von Monika und Claus Arndt stapeln sich die Lernhefte des heimischen Verlags. Alles ist handproduziert, das ist das Markenzeichen des Verlags. FOTOS: ASTRID SCHMIDHUBER

Die Hefte des Durchblicker-Verlags: Insgesamt 58 Lerntrainer haben die Arndts schon herausgebracht.

Am besten verkaufen sich die Lerntrainer für Grundschule und 5. und 6. Klasse

Als die Arndts die Bücher in immer größerer Stückzahl verkauften, stellte sich die Frage, wie sie die Lerntrainer weiter produzieren wollen. Sie entschieden sich, die Bücher selbst zu drucken. „Alles ist handproduziert, das ist unser Markenzeichen", sagt Monika Arndt.

Sie legen Wert darauf, dass ihre Aufgaben schulnah sind und so auch wirklich abgefragt werden könnten. „Außerdem ist es wichtig für uns, die Schüler für das Lernen zu motivieren. Häufig schreiben Kinder schlechte Noten, weil sie zu wenig Selbstvertrauen haben", sagt Claus Arndt. „Wenn die Kinder mit unseren Schultrainern lernen, erkennen sie Aufgaben aus dem Unterricht wieder, das gibt ihnen ein Erfolgserlebnis und motiviert sie." Natürlich könnten die Bücher keine schon vorher entstandenen Wissenslücken schließen, „aber sie helfen, zu vertiefen und zu wiederholen."

AKTUELLES IN KÜRZE

38-Jähriger stirbt nach Drogenkonsum

Ein 38-jähriger Münchner ist am vergangenen Freitag an den Folgen von Kokain- und Alkoholkonsum gestorben. Nach Angaben der Polizei wurde der arbeitslose Münchner am Donnerstag, 17. November, in eine Klinik eingeliefert. Dort musste er reanimiert werden. In seinem Urin wurde ein hoher Kokaingehalt festgestellt. Zudem hatte er eine Alkoholvergiftung. Die Obduktion ergab, dass der 38-Jährige an einer Überdosis Rauschgift gestorben war. Die Polizei schließt Fremdverschulden aus. pim

Rechte und Pflichten von Mietern

Viele Auseinandersetzungen zwischen Vermietern und Mietern resultieren daraus, dass die Parteien ihre Rechte und Pflichten nicht kennen oder diese falsch einschätzen. Die Rechtsanwältin Gisela Weber vom Mieterverein München erläutert bei einem Infoabend im Bauzentrum München, Willy-Brandt-Allee 10, am Dienstag, 13. Dezember, ab 18 Uhr, welche Klauseln Mieter vor der Unterzeichnung eines Formularmietvertrages besonders unter die Lupe nehmen sollten. Sie spricht außerdem die Probleme des Alltags an, die im täglichen Umgang zwischen den Mietvertragsparteien und den Nachbarn auftreten können. Der Eintritt ist frei. do